CONTENTS

Decorating your home with your own creations is a most enjoyable and satisfying experience. If this is your first attempt at making a decorator item, you're in for a treat. Start with the projects labeled "Beginner simple." You will find the instructions in this book easy to follow. The items are fun to make and the results will be fabulous. If you have some creative experience, you'll enjoy the challenge of the more detailed projects. These are the same designs sold under "My Country Garden" label in gift shops in Northern California.

All of the required materials, in a variety of colors to suit your home, should be readily available from your local craft store. You will find your projects will be easier to make when you use a hot glue gun. Now pick one of the projects in this book, follow the easy directions, add plenty of tender loving care, and be ready for the compliments!

Enjoy!

Judi

Summer's Joy

Nothing could be more lovely than the look of fresh picked garden flowers gathered in an array of twigs and ribbons.

MATERIALS NEEDED

2 large silk roses for the focal point
1 medium silk rose in a dark color
11 stems of long slender silk flowers such as the lilac used here
3 clusters of deep color tiny silk daisies
3 clusters of light color tiny silk daisies
7 stems of light colored silk flowers on wispy stems
7 stems of silk rose leaves
7 stems of silk ivy
5 stems of silk green leaves for filler
1 bird and nest
1 bundle of long twigs (such as birch twigs)
3 1/2 yards of wired ribbon
Small amount of Spanish moss and wire

INSTRUCTIONS

1. Arrange the longest twigs in two small bundles. Place the base end of each bundle together and overlap slightly. Make sure the twigs extend out to the length you want the garland to be when completed. Wire and hot glue these bundles together to form your base (see illustration #1). Cover the wire with Spanish moss and form a loop of wire in the center for hanging.

Illustration #1

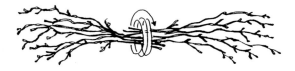

2. Glue into each side of this base three long slender stems of lilac (or similar flower). Cut the stems at various lengths for a pleasing look.

3. Place the birds nest on top of the base in the center and glue firmly in place. Glue in the moss and bird.

4. Place the focal point roses at the front lower left and upper right and glue into the base.

5. Tuck the dark rose in at the base of the nest and glue.

6. Place more moss around the base of the nest to fill in and glue in green leaves to form the background.

7. Tuck in the dark and light daisies on each side of your arrangement and glue to hold.

8. Add wispy twigs up and out from the base both top and bottom. Glue to hold in place.

9. Glue in the rose leaves, ivy, wispy stem flowers and long slender lilac extending out from the base in a free flowing manner.

10. Twist and curl the wired ribbon from one end of your arrangement to the other.

This striking garland will captivate the attention of all who visit your home!

English Flower Garden

Your room will feel like an English country garden when you add this wonderful floral wreath.

MATERIALS NEEDED

Large wreath (photo shows a 24")
2 Large silk roses in a dark color
3 stems of long, slender silk flowers
3 stems of small silk flowers in a dark color
(add depth to your arrangement)
3 stems of silk rose leaves
1 long stem of dried plumosis fern (optional)
1 large bird and nest
2 tiny birds
1 yard or wired ribbon
Small amounts of spanish moss, twigs, statice, peppergrass,
latifolia or any other filler flowers
in colors to compliment the silk flowers

INSTRUCTIONS

1. Glue moss to the bottom front of the wreath, extending slightly up the left side.

2. Wire and hot glue the birds nest on wreath half-way up the left side.

3. Cut the stems of the three long slender silk flowers at different lengths and glue into the wreath (see illustration #1).

4. Glue in the two roses and three stems of the deep color flowers as shown in the illustration.

Illustration #1

5. Glue the dried filler flowers into the wreath in clusters to fill behind and around the silk flowers.

6. Place a small amount of moss and the large bird into the nest and glue in place. Glue twigs around the nest and through the arrangement.

7. Tuck in one long stem of rose leaves behind the nest and up the left side to the top of the wreath and glue to hold. Cut off clusters of leaves and place throughout the arrangement.

8. Glue the long stem of plumosis fern into the arrangement on the left. Twist the fern over the front and up the right side of the wreath. Glue the tiny bird to the wreath on the upper right side.

9. For the final touch, twist and curl the wired ribbon into your arrangement, beginning at the bottom and proceeding up the left side. Glue to hold in place.

Enjoy!

Home Sweet Home

This adorable bird cage will look perfect in any room in your home.

MATERIALS NEEDED

A bird cage any style you like (you can spray paint it yourself)
4 clusters of silk lilacs or any flower that is long and slender
1 stem of silk roses (mine had one bud fully opened,
another slightly smaller, and a tight bud)
2 stems of silk ivy
2 1/2 yards of wired ribbon
1 large bird and 1 tiny bird
Small amount of Spanish moss, oasis, twigs,
and a small cluster of any flowers

INSTRUCTIONS

1. Hot glue a small piece of oasis to the very top of the bird cage. Glue moss over the oasis to completely conceal. Glue moss to the bottom of the cage. (Hint: If the cage has large open slats, cover a piece of cardboard with moss and glue to the bottom of the cage). Tuck a cluster of flowers into the moss at the bottom of the cage.

2. Glue the twigs into the oasis. Let them twist and turn down the left side and a few on top and to the right side for a natural effect. Bring one through the side and into the middle of the cage as a perch. Glue the large bird onto the perch and the tiny bird onto one of the twig branches on the right side. (Hint: Place some moss under the birds to hide the glue).

3. Glue the ivy stems onto the oasis, following the line of the twigs. Cut a few ivy leaves to glue onto the door.

4. Glue in the long slender flowers. Let three of them cascade down the right side (this balances the twigs and ivy on the left). Drape one stem over the top of the cage on the left.

5. Make a tie tow with large loops (see instructions on page 33) and glue onto the top at a slight angle (see photo). Cascade the ribbon down through the ivy and twigs on the left side. Bring it through the side of the cage, so the end of the ribbon is inside, and glue to hold. Cut two pieces of ribbon 6" in length and tuck under the bow in front and back. Glue in place and cut all ribbon ends in a "V" shape.

6. Glue the large rose into the ivy on the top right side, and the medium rose on the left. Place the rose bud under the large rose. Glue in rose leaves.

This darling bird cage will become the focal point of your room. Enjoy!

Robin's Roost

Add a charming touch to your garden with a darling bird house.

MATERIALS NEEDED

Find a cute bird house or make one yourself
Look for a wrought iron stand at a flea market or place the bird house on a wooden post
3 small stems of silk ivy
1 large bird (optional)
1 yard of grosgrain ribbon (or any ribbon that can be used outdoors)
Small amounts of spanish moss, twigs, and oasis or foam.

INSTRUCTIONS

1. Hot glue a small piece of oasis on the top of the roof to the rear of the birdhouse. Glue on spanish moss to cover the oasis and let it cascade down the side of the roof.

2. Glue the twigs into the oasis and let them twist out and down the left side. Glue in the ivy stem and a little extra moss on top and in the front opening. Glue on the bird.

3. Make a tie bow (following instructions on page 33) and tuck in under the bird.

Perch the bird house on a stand or post in your garden and enjoy all summer!

Floral Symphony

A gleaming glass hurricane filled with potpourri and embellished with beautiful flowers will add a fabulous touch to your home.

MATERIALS NEEDED

A glass hurricane any size you like (a 16" hurricane was used here)
1 extra large bag of potpourri
Oasis or form board to form a center core inside the glass
1 large silk rose as a focal point
5 stems of long slender silk flowers such as lavender lilac
2 light colored silk carnations or other similar size flowers
2 dark colored silk bachelor buttons or similar size as carnation
2 medium size silk roses and 3 rose buds
2 stems of silk rose leaves
1 stem of silk ivy
1 tiny bird and nest
1 yard of wired ribbon
2 yards of tiny satin ribbon in contrasting color
$^1/_2$ yard decorative braid
Small amount of Spanish moss and twigs

INSTRUCTIONS

1. Cut oasis or foam in a circle to fit inside the bottom of the glass hurricane. Glue in place. Glue decorative braid around the outside of the glass to hide the foam edge. Green felt glued to the bottom of the foam will prevent scratching your furniture.

2. Cut a long slender piece of oasis or foam to fit down the middle of the hurricane, leaving enough space on the sides for a thin layer of potpourri. Glue to the base piece of foam. Allow the oasis to extend beyond the top of the glass approximately 4". (You may have to glue several pieces together to achieve this length.)

3. Pour the potpourri into the glass around the oasis core. Gently tap the glass on the table to allow the potpourri to pack down. When you have filled the glass, tuck in a few pieces of oasis around the top to hold the potpourri in place. Cover all the oasis at the top with Spanish moss and glue to hold. Let the moss cascade slightly over the top of the vase.

4. Glue 2 stems of long slender flowers into the oasis by extending one upward and another cascading down the front to the left. Glue a few twigs into the oasis on the left side of the arrangement, extending upward to achieve the desired height.

5. Glue the large focal point rose into the oasis, center front. Glue in the medium size rose and two rose buds slightly lower on the right side. Let the rose buds extend out and down.

6. Tuck in one light colored carnation under the medium rose and let it extend down with the rose buds. Glue in a stem of ivy, allowing it to cascade down the right side.

7. Glue the nest to the top of the oasis on the right side and fill with moss. Sprinkle potpourri on top and glue a tiny bird to the edge.

8. Tuck in one dark colored bachelor button flower at the base of the nest on the right side. Place another on the top just behind the nest to the left.

9. Glue one light colored carnation, one medium size rose and one rose bud to the left of the nest.

10. Fill in between the flowers with rose leaves and twigs. Be sure to place some twigs extending down the right side for a wispy effect.

11. Make a tie bow, follow instructions on Page 34, and glue into your arrangement on the right. Let the ends gently twist and curl down. Twist and curl the tiny satin ribbon throughout your arrangement and glue to hold in place. Attach three long tiny satin ribbons to the base of your bow. Tie "Love" knots at the ends for a great finish.

Enjoy!

In the Garden

Bring the garden indoors with this beautiful floral wreath complete with a mama bird tending her nest. (I like to put three eggs in the nest to represent my three children). This wreath will look great in any room in your home so choose the colors that suit your decor, and have a fun time creating!

MATERIALS NEEDED

18″ wreath in natural or white (you can spray paint it any color you like)
3 long slender silk flowers—2 light colored and 1 darker
6 small silk flowers in a dark complementary color
1 small cluster of silk flowers in a dark color
2 small vines of ivy
small amount of the following...
german statice—spanish moss—dried filler flower such as caspia or latafolia—pussy willow—twigs
1 bird and nest—eggs optional
6 yards of untwisted paper ribbon
wire

INSTRUCTIONS

1. Glue on spanish moss to the bottom front of the wreath, extending slightly up the side to the left.

2. Make a bow per instructions on page 34. This bow has five loops on each side about 4″ long. Tie the bow with ribbon cut 20″ long. Leave these ends long and cut on the diagonal.

3. Wire and glue the bow in place just to the left of the bottom center.

4. Cut a 36″ length of ribbon. Glue one end under the bow on the top left side, wave and curl the ribbon up the side. Secure with glue as you go.

Cut a 30″ length of ribbon and glue one end under the bow on the right bottom side. Wave and curl the ribbon along the bottom of the wreath, securing with glue as you go. Cut ends on the diagonal. (*see illustration #1 for step 4 and 5*)

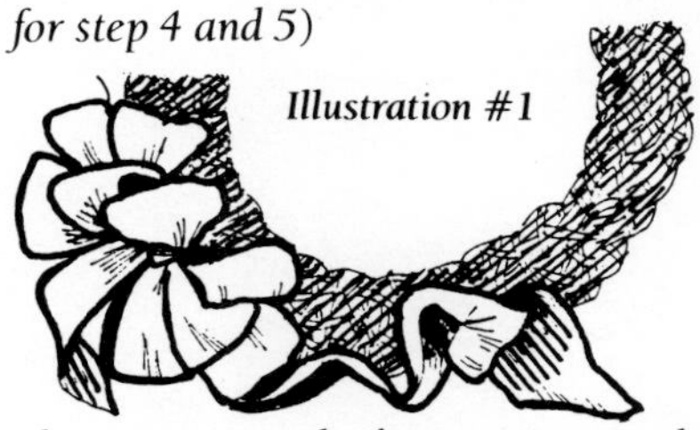

Illustration #1

6. Tuck the nest in on the bottom just to the right of center. Wire down and hot glue to secure. Glue spanish moss around the base and inside of the nest.

7. Glue in the three long slender silk flowers, cutting stems at three different heights. Place the darker flower in the middle of the grouping and the lighter flowers on each side. (*see illustration #2*). You can cut some of the blooms off the bottom of these flowers to be used later.

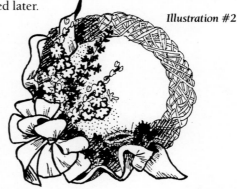

Illustration #2

8. Glue the dried filler flower and german statice into the wreath in clusters...making it very full going up the left side and tapering off to the nest. Add a small amount below and to the right of the nest.

9. Glue in the pussy willow, twigs, ivy and other flowers. You will create a more natural look by layering these instead of placing in a straight row.

10. Glue in mama bird and eggs. Enjoy!

Reflections

Complete the charming look to your bedroom or bath with this sweet rosebud mirror. This is surprisingly simple to make and something you're sure to enjoy.

MATERIALS NEEDED

framed mirror any size you like (this one is white wicker 18″ × 13″)
8 silk rosebuds
2–3 yards untwisted paper ribbon
2–3 yards ⅛″ wide satin ribbon
small amount of german statice
wire

INSTRUCTIONS

1. Make a paper ribbon bow as per instruction on page 34. This bow has three loops on each side about 3″ long. Cut the tail even with the end of the loop. Tie the bow with a 12″ length of ribbon, pulling one end up and the other down.

2. Hot glue the bow to the frame on the upper left side.

3. Cut a 24″ length of paper ribbon. Glue one end of the ribbon behind the bow on the left side. Wave and curl down the left side of the mirror, gluing in place as you go.

4. Cut an 18″ length of paper ribbon and glue one end in behind the bow on the right side. Wave and curl across the top of the mirror, gluing in place as you go. Cut ends of the ribbon diagonally.

5. Glue the german statice onto the frame in clusters, extending from behind the bow on each side to the end of the paper ribbon.

6. Glue five rosebuds on the left side and three rosebuds on the right side of the bow. *(see illustration #1)* Cut off leaves of the rosebuds and glue in place as you like.

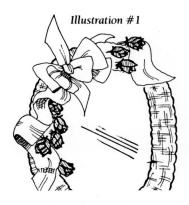

Illustration #1

7. Cut six lengths of ⅛″ satin ribbon about 5″ long. Glue one of these ribbons around each of the loops of the paper ribbon bow.

8. Cut two lengths of ⅛″ satin ribbon 24″ long. Glue one end of each ribbon under the left side of the bow. Wave and curl both ribbons around the rosebuds on the left side of the mirror, gluing in place as you go.

9. Cut one length of ⅛″ satin ribbon 18″ long. Glue the end under the bow on the right side and wave and curl through the rosebuds, gluing in place as you go.

10. Cut three lengths of ⅛″ satin ribbon 4″ long and glue to the bottom center of the bow.

Now stand back and look at this darling mirror you just created. Have fun finding just the perfect spot in your home for all to enjoy!

Feather My Nest

B ring a smile to those you love as they enjoy this tiny bird nestled in the lovely magnolia twig bundle. You can buy a nest or use one you've found outside. Place it on a coffee table and be ready to make more, as all of your friends will want one too! This is a fun, easy to make project.

MATERIALS NEEDED

1 large silk magnolia with bud

3 yards of untwisted paper ribbon

1 bird and nest—eggs optional

small amount of spanish moss

twigs

small amount of dried filler flower such as caspia or german statice

1 large lotus pod

wire

INSTRUCTIONS

1. Arrange the twigs in a bundle and wrap with wire at the stem end.

2. Wire the twigs and magnolia together at the base of the flower. Leave one end of the wire sticking up about 4″. Secure the bundle with hot glue.

3. Tuck the birds nest in next to the back of the flower. Pull the 4″ piece of wire up and back down through the bottom of the nest and twist end around the twigs. Glue to secure in place.

4. Glue spanish moss around the base of the nest and around the twigs to hide the wire.

5. Glue small amount of spanish moss inside the nest. Cut the wire on feet of the bird ½″ long and glue into the nest. Glue in eggs if you like.

6. Tuck the lotus pod into the base of the nest and flower. Glue firmly in place.

7. Glue dried filler flowers and small twigs around the base of the magnolia.

8. Make a bow from paper ribbon as per instructions on page 34. This bow has three loops on each side about 5″ long. Leave the tail on the bow 12″ long. Cut one length of paper ribbon 26″ long and tie around the center of the bow. Pull all three ends down and cut on the diagonal. Glue onto the twigs at the base of the nest.

I'm sure you had fun making this project for your home.
This book has many other ideas for you to try.

French Country Elegance

This elegant wreath will give your home a "French country" look and be the focal point of any room. Place it in the living room over your fireplace or sofa, or over your bed or dresser...anywhere you need something fantastic. It's sure to capture the attention of your guests and what fun to tell them you made it yourself! Choose the colors that enhance your home and go to it!

MATERIALS NEEDED

Large vine wreath, spray painted off-white (this one is 24" across. If you can't find one that large, go with what you find.)
3 large silk magnolia blossoms
14 small silk flowers, light in color
7 small silk flowers, dark in color (dark colors are needed to give depth and dimension to your work)
6 branches silk ficus leaf or ivy
1 bunch dried filler flower such as caspia or latafolia
spanish moss
twigs
3 lotus pods
bird
6 yards untwisted paper ribbon
wire

INSTRUCTIONS

1. Make bow per instructions on page 34. This bow has five loops on each side about 6" long. Cut tail of bow even with end of loops. Tie the bow with a 36" length of ribbon, pulling one end up and the other down.

2. Wire and glue the bow to the left side of the wreath almost to the top. Hold firmly in place until glue sets.

3. Cut one length of ribbon 47" long. Glue one end under the bow at the top and loop ribbon around wreath across the top. Glue in place as you go.

4. Cut another length of ribbon 26" long and glue one end under the bottom side of the bow. Loop ribbon around the wreath down the side. Glue in place as you go. Cut ribbon ends on the diagonal. You can curl the tie ends of the bow by wrapping tightly around a pencil.

5. Glue spanish moss along the bottom front and slightly up the sides of the wreath.

6. Make a round birds nest out of spanish moss and glue it in the center on the bottom of the wreath. Glue three lotus pods to the right and under the nest. (*see illustration #1*)

7. Glue on the three large magnolia blossoms. (*see illustration #1*)

Illustration #1

8. Glue on dried filler flower such as caspia or latafolia. Make it full on the left side, tapering down to the nest, and then coming out to the right side of the nest and pods.

9. Glue on the light and dark silk flowers to the right and left of the nest. (*see photo*)

10. Glue in the ficus or ivy leaves and twigs.

11. Cut the wire on the feet of the bird ½" long and glue securely into the nest.

12. Cut one length of ribbon 9" long and glue in just to the left of the nest. Cut another length of ribbon 6" long and glue in behind the magnolia on right. Cut the ends of the ribbons on the diagonal.

Victorian Rose

This dainty victorian rosebud wreath will look wonderful in your bathroom or bedroom. Your little girl will surely want one over her bed. This wreath is so easy to do, you could make them for gifts!

MATERIALS NEEDED

8–10″ round vine wreath

6 silk rosebuds

1 bunch of light colored small silk flowers

6 yards 1″ wide moire or satin ribbon, light in color

5 yards ⅛″ wide satin ribbon in a darker color

5 yards lace ribbon

*small amounts of spanish moss, german statice,
and peppergrass*

wire

INSTRUCTIONS

1. Glue a small amount of spanish moss across the bottom front of the wreath to form a backing for the bow and flowers.

2. Make a bow using the lace and two sizes of ribbon together per instructions on page 34. This bow has 5 loops on each side, each about 3″ long. Leave the tail on the bow 15″ long. Tie the bow with ribbons cut 36″ long. Pull all the ends of the ribbons down and leave as long streamers. Cut each end on the diagonal. Wire and glue the bow onto the wreath on top of the spanish moss.

3. Cut a length of ribbon 46″ long. Glue one end of the ribbon behind the bow and wrap it evenly around the wreath, securing with glue as you wrap, until you return to the bow. Tuck the loose end of the ribbon in behind the bow and secure with glue.

4. Glue the german statice and the peppergrass onto the wreath behind each side of the bow.

5. Glue three rosebuds on each side among the statice and peppergrass. Cut off the rose leaves if desired, and glue them into the wreath to help fill in the arrangement.

6. Glue three small clusters of light colored silk flowers around each side of the bow.

Now find the ideal place to hang your wreath and admire your handiwork.

Glorious Garland

You'll enjoy the lush look of this flower garland in your home. Place it over a door, china hutch, fireplace, or bed...anywhere you want a beautiful floral look!

MATERIALS NEEDED

6 yards of untwisted paper ribbon
6 long slender silk flowers:
(4 light-colored and 2 in a darker shade)
12–14 small white silk flowers
6 small flowers in a dark complementary color
4 small silk ivy vines
1 bunch dried filler flower such as latafolia
or caspia—anything with long stems
small amount of spanish moss
wire

INSTRUCTIONS

1. Arrange the long stems of dried filler flower in two bundles exactly the same. Make bundles full in the middle and taper out to very slender ends about 24″ long.

2. Wrap wire around each bundle...then wire the stem ends together, overlapping about 8″. *(Refer to illustration below in Petite French Bundle.)* Reinforce wire with hot glue. Cover with spanish moss glued to the front and back to hide the wire and form the base.

3. Make paper ribbon bow as per instructions on page 34. This bow has five loops on each side about 4½″ long. Cut the tail even with the end of loops. Tie with a 14″ length of ribbon. Pull one end of tie up to top and cut 9″ long. Pull the other end down and cut 10″ long (these ends are cut on the diagonal).

4. Attach the bow to the center of the garland with wire and hot glue. Hold firmly in place until glue sets.

5. Glue the long slender silk flowers to the base in behind the bow on each side...placing the darker ones in the center and bending to shape, extending to the ends of the garland. Cut the lighter ones slightly shorter, and glue on each side of the darker flower.

6. Glue in the ivy and white and dark flowers to accent as you like.

7. Cut two lengths of paper ribbon, each 36″ long. Firmly glue one end of each of these ribbons behind the bow on either side, holding until glue sets. Twist the ribbon through the garland of flowers on each side to the tip end. Glue at different points on the back side of the garland to hold the ribbon in place. Cut ribbon ends on the diagonal.

8. Glue in dried filler flowers in a pleasing fashion to make garland as full as you like.

Petite French Bundle

This tiny twig and flower bundle is darling just about anywhere in your home. It is so easy to make that you can do several at a time for gifts!

MATERIALS NEEDED

6 small silk flowers in dark colors
6 small silk flowers in off-white colors
6 small clusters of tiny silk flowers in light colors
small amounts of the following . . . twigs, spanish moss, and german statice
1 yard of 2½" wide ribbon
wire

INSTRUCTIONS

1. Arrange the twigs in two bundles that are the exact same size (each about 11" long).

2. Wrap wire around each bundle . . . then wire the stem ends together, overlapping about 2". (*see illustration #1*) Hot glue to secure.

3. Glue the spanish moss all around the center of the two connected bundles to hide the wire.

4. The bow is made with two loops each 3½" long and wired securely in the middle. Cut the bow tail even with the end of loop. Tie the bow with a length of ribbon cut 18" long, pulling both ends down. Cut ends on the diagonal.

5. Wire and glue the bow to the center of the twig bundle.

6. Glue the german statice to the front of the twigs behind each side of the bow. Extend the german statice out about ½ way to the end of the twigs.

7. Glue three silk flowers of each color into the twigs on each side of the bow. Don't be afraid to cut off some of the leaves and glue them where needed. Also glue in extra twigs for fullness.

Illustration #1

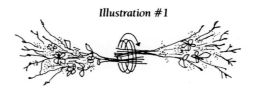

Simply Bows

*Y*our own special personality flair will be visible in your home when you add something you have created yourself. A simple bow that you have made from beautiful ribbon can bring that final touch to just about anything.

This chapter will give you easy to follow instructions on how to embellish a gift package, floral arrangement, picture frames, curtains and an unexpected flair to your dining room chandelier. I have also included some decorator accents for your home using a few yards of beautiful ribbon and a touch of flowers.

Enjoy!

Judi

Party Bows

CHANDELIER

*D*ecorate your chandelier to create a festive mood or compliment a vase of flowers with a bow tucked in for extra flair. Use red ribbon at Christmas, lavender and pink for Easter . . . let your creativity flow!

MATERIALS NEEDED

10 yards of 1½" florists ribbon
Florists wire

INSTRUCTIONS

Make two large Basic Bows *see page 34* with 5 loops on each side, and make the tail 30" long. Secure with wire, leaving the ends long. Ribbon tie ends can be left as long as you like. Wire the bows back-to-back on each side of the chandelier chain at the ceiling. Add extra streamers if you like by just putting ribbon through the chandelier chain under the bow.

FLOWER BOW

MATERIALS NEEDED

6 yards of 1½" florists ribbon
Florists wire

INSTRUCTIONS

Make a Basic Bow *see page 34*. This bow has 5 loops on each side. Cut tail on bow to a length of 30". Leave tie end approximately 1 yard long. Leave ends of wire long enough to place inside vase to hold the bow in position. Cut the tie ribbon 2 yards long and cascade the tie ends down the vase and onto the table. Cut ends on the diagonal.

Cut-Ups

A bright paper bursting with color that has a small size pattern is all you need to decorate a delightful gift box.

MATERIALS NEEDED

Colorful wrapping paper with a small design
Bright ribbon
Glue

INSTRUCTIONS

1. Wrap your package, setting aside a few scraps of paper.

2. Tie the ribbon around the box with the knot in the front. Make a bow with three loops on each side about 3" long, cut tail end even with the loops. Tie the bow onto the package with a length of ribbon cut 14". (See bow instructions on page 34).

3. Cut out the designs you want to highlight from the scraps of wrapping paper. Glue the cutouts to the end of the loops on the bow. Super!

Free Flowing Bow

This darling flowing bow will add a special touch to any room in your home. This simple-to-make bow can be made in any size to suit your needs.

MATERIALS NEEDED

3–4 yards of untwisted paper ribbon
Florists wire
Hot glue

INSTRUCTIONS

Make Basic Bow described on page 34, with 5 loops on each side. Leave the tail of the bow 18″ long. Tie the bow with a length of ribbon cut 24″ long. Cut the ends on a diagonal. Glue in extra bow tails to the back of the bow of various lengths, making five altogether (*see photo for placement*). Attach the bow to the wall. Arrange the ribbon ends in a pleasing manner by simply tacking them in place with tiny nails hidden in the folds, or use masking tape on the back of the ribbon.

This darling flowing bow will add a special touch to any room in your home.

Picture Ribbon

Your treasured pictures will become a focal point when you hang them from this elegant picture ribbon.

MATERIALS NEEDED

*4 yards Morie satin ribbon
(or velvet would work nicely)
1 piece florists wire
Hot glue gun*

INSTRUCTIONS

Follow instructions for the Basic Bow on page 34, making three loops on each side. Cut the tail of ribbon even with the end of the loop. Secure with wire, leaving the ends long. Tie the bow with a length of ribbon making sure that the longer end will accommodate your pictures (ours pictured is 1 yard long). Pull the short end up and pull the long end down. Trim by cutting two pointed ends. Hot glue back to hold in place. Twist the wire ends to form a small loop in back of the bow for hanging on the wall. Attach the pictures to the ribbon by hand sewing on through hooks in back of the frames or by placing tiny nails through the ribbon into the wall.

Curtain Tie Backs

Complete the charming look to your window by simply tying on a beautiful bow. Use lace to give that feminine Victorian touch or velvet to add an elegant feeling. The selections of ribbon are endless to capture the look that best enhances your home.

MATERIALS NEEDED

2¹/₂ - 3 yards of moire satin ribbon
3 - 3¹/₂ yards of lace were used in the window pictured.
To determine your needs, decide how long you want the ribbon ends to be and how wide across you want the bow.

INSTRUCTIONS

Hold the ribbon and lace together as you make the bow. Follow the Tie Bow instructions below.

Tie Bow

A simple bow made from beautiful ribbon can add that wonderful final touch to almost everything. You can wrap a gift with great wrapping paper but it doesn't look complete until you embellish it with a bow. The final touch on a little girl's dress is the big bow sash in back! If you've tried to tie that "perfect" bow but somehow it doesn't seem to look quite right, don't give up. Follow the instructions below, and practice. In no time your friends will be asking for instructions from you!

INSTRUCTIONS

1. Starting with both ends even, cross the right ribbon underneath the left (this is a very important to keep the bow straight). Make a half-knot as shown in illustration #1.

Illustration #1

2. With left hand, make a loop between the thumb and index finger, keeping the wrong sides of the ribbon together. Cross over the top of the loop with the other ribbon right side up. Now finish the second loop by pulling it up through the center space you've just created. Pull tight.

(HINT: To prevent the wrong side out on the second loop, twist ribbon a half-turn just before sending it up through the center space (see illustration #2). If the right tail is wrong side out, twist the left loop and the right tail towards you simultaneously in a rolling motion.

Illustration #2

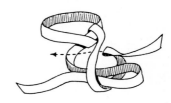

Garland Bow

What a fantastic decorator statement you will make with this beautiful garland of bows. This is a fun, easy and inexpensive way to decorate a large area over your bed, sofa, fireplace mantel, doorway . . . anyplace that needs something special.

MATERIALS NEEDED

9 - 10 yards of untwisted paper ribbon
2 pieces florists wire
Hot glue

INSTRUCTIONS

Simply make two large Basic Bows (see instructions below), making 5 loops on each side. Cut the tail on the bow 20" long. Cut a length of ribbon 25" long to tie bow. Pull short end up and long end down. Cut the ends on a diagonal. Cut two equal lengths of paper ribbon to form the garland between the bows (ours pictured is 1¾ yards each). Place these lengths of ribbon together and hot glue the ends to the back of each bow. Hang the bows close enough together that the garland has a gentle swag.

Basic Bow

This bow can be tricky to make if this is your first attempt. The secret is to practice, so don't give up if the bow slips out of your hand and you have to start over. My first bow was a disaster but I kept trying until I finally made a perfect bow. You can do it too . . . just follow these simple instructions.

INSTRUCTIONS

1. Hold the ribbon right side up between your thumb and index finger. Pinch the ribbon approximately 2" from the end and then form a loop as large as you need, rolling the ribbon up and away from you. Place the long end of the ribbon between your thumb and index finger to create the bow's center (see illustration #1).

Illustration #1

2. Before making the bottom loop, make a half twist to the left so that the ribbon will be right side out, then roll the ribbon down and away from you. Pinch the ribbon together at the bow's center (see illustration #2).

Illustration #2

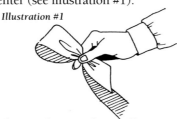

3. Continue making the loops until the desired number is reached, keeping the loop sizes the same. Remember to ALWAYS pinch the ribbon at the center and to ALWAYS twist to the left before forming each loop.
   HINT: To keep the bow from slipping, lift your index finger as you twist, momentarily using your middle finger and thumb to secure the loops until the twist is completed.

4. Once the loops are completed, cut the end of the ribbon leaving a tail as long as required (this length will vary on each design). Now you are ready to wire.

5. To secure the bow, tie a piece of wire around the bow's center and twist the wire ends tightly together underneath the bow. Now arrange the loops to form a perfect bow.

6. Cut a length of ribbon (exact size will be given in each design instructions) to create your "tie" for the bow. Wrap the tie around the bow's center to conceal the florists wire and knot the ribbon in the back.

7. All ends of the ribbon should be cut on the diagonal.

Sweet Hanging Bow

This adorable bow looks wonderful just about anywhere a tender touch is needed.

MATERIALS NEEDED

3 yards untwisted paper ribbon
2 yards tiny satin ribbon
Florists wire
Small amount of dried or silk flowers
1 small bird
1 small pinecone or pod

INSTRUCTIONS

Follow the instructions for the Basic Bow on page 34, making 3 loops on each side. Leave a tail on the bow 12" long. Tie the bow with a length of ribbon cut 18" long. Pull one end up and the other down. Cut the ends on a diagonal. Glue small loops and streamers of tiny satin ribbon into the completed bow (see picture for placement). Glue a small pinecone or pod into the center of the bow. Glue an assortment of dried and silk flowers around the pinecone (see photo). Hang this bow by a length of tiny satin ribbon glued to the back of the bow. Add a little bird to make this bow absolutely charming.

Graduated Loop Bow

INSTRUCTIONS

This bow is made exactly the same as the BASIC BOW except when making the loops. The loops on this bow are *not* the same size. Each row of loops should gradually be larger until the desired number is reached. Wire and tie the same as BASIC BOW instructions..

Florists Bow

INSTRUCTIONS

1. This bow is made exactly the same as the BASIC BOW except begin by pinching the ribbon between your thumb and index finger 4" from the end.

2. Proceed with the instructions for the BASIC BOW until all the desired loops are formed. Before you secure the bow with wire, twist the 4" end on top of the bow, making sure the right side is out. Curl this end around and place it under your thumb. Place the wire through the small center loop, taking care to catch the end in the center loop (see illustration #1).

Illustration #1

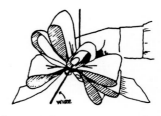

3. Arrange loops to form a perfect bow. Cut a length of ribbon to create your "tie" for the bow. Place the tie ribbon through this small center loop and knot in the back.

Christmas

Oh, how I love Christmas! The festivities begin for our family the day after Thanksgiving when we go off into the Santa Cruz mountains and cut the most beautiful Christmas Tree we can find. The fragrance of fresh cut pine inspires us to dress our home for Christmas. Traditions are so important to a family; ours begins when we decorate our tree and place the tiny nativity scene tenderly under the branches. It's a time to let the child in all of us come alive, a time to reminisce, a time to create fond memories.

Decorating your home with your own creations is so rewarding. The ideas shown in this section are fresh and exciting, yet warm and inviting. You will find the instructions easy to follow, the items fun to make and the results will be fantastic!

Enjoy!

Judi

Home for Christmas

You will love the natural woodsy look of this beautiful Christmas arrangement, complete with a Mama and Papa bird nestled in the greenery.

MATERIALS NEEDED

*one large natural twig basket with a handle
(the one in the photo is 12" across)
7 long full branches of artificial pine
6 branches of preserved cedar
7 large pine cones
7 large artificial ivy leaves
9 berry clusters
1 small bunch of latafolia
twigs
2 birds—tiny bird eggs optional
2½ yards of ⅛" ribbon
tiny pine cones
small amount of Spanish moss
two blocks of oasis for dried arrangements*

INSTRUCTIONS

1. Cut the oasis to snugly fit into your basket and glue to the bottom.

2. Cover the oasis with Spanish moss and glue in place.

3. Glue five of the long, full pine branches firmly into the oasis (see illustration #1).

4. Glue all large pine cones securely in place (see illustration #1).

Illustration #1

5. Cut the remaining pine branches into varying lengths (about 5"–8"), and glue into the oasis around the pine cones, filling in the center area.

6. Glue long stems of preserved cedar and latafolia on the left side, and the shorter pieces on the right side and into the center of your arrangement (see illustration #2)

Illustration #2

7. Glue in the berries using the photo for placement.

8. Glue the twigs slightly to the left of the center (see photo for placement).

9. Make a small birds nest from the Spanish moss and glue it into the arrangement just to the right of center front.

10. Tuck in the tiny pine cones to fill in the arrangement and have some spill over the edge on the front left side.

11. Arrange the ivy and holly leaves to the right of the center and tuck some in around the birds nest, following the flow of the pine branches off to the right. Sprinkle a few leaves to the left of center in the front. Glue all leaves in place.

12. Glue the "Mama" bird into the Spanish moss nest. Glue in the tiny eggs if you like (I placed three eggs in a nest to represent my three children). Glue a small amount of Spanish moss to the basket handle just to the right of center. Tuck the "Papa" bird into the moss on the handle and glue securely in place.

13. Make a small bow following instructions on page 34. This bow has three loops on each side about 2½" long. Cut the tail end about 7" long. Tie the bow with ribbon cut 14" long. Pull all ends down and glue bow to the center of the basket (see photo). Use the remaining ribbon to connect the two birds. Glue one end under the beak of the bird on the handle. Twist and curl the ribbon down to the bird in the nest and glue the end under the beak.

Enjoy!

Christmas Welcome

J̵ay Merry Christmas to your friends when they come to your home, by hanging this beautiful wreath on your front door. The gold bells will sound a friendly jingle as the door opens to welcome your guests.

MATERIALS NEEDED

*20″ pine wreath—artificial or natural
2 stems of artificial ivy
3 stems of berries
5 full pieces of preserved cedar
4 stems of latafolia or other filler flower branches
6 yards of ribbon 2½″ wide
(I used wired ribbon to achieve the curling effect)
2 yards of ½″ wide ribbon for bells
(if you can't find the same ribbon as the bow, you
can use plain red or green)
small amounts of Spanish moss and twigs
red bird
5 large gold jingle bells
florists wire*

INSTRUCTIONS

1. Make bow following instructions on page 34. This bow has five loops on each side about 5″ long. Cut the tail ends even with the end of the loops. Tie the bow with ribbon cut 20″ long, pulling one end up and the other end down. Leave these ends long and cut in a V shape.

2. Wire and glue the bow onto the top center of the wreath.

3. Cut a 17″ length of ribbon and glue one end under the bottom of the bow. Cut a 10″ length of ribbon and glue one end under the bow on the right side. Cut another length of ribbon 10″ long and glue one end under the bow on the left side. Cut all ends to a V shape. If you are using wired ribbon as I did, you can curl the ends around a wooden spoon handle and gently pull to loosen (arrange as shown in the photo). If you are not using wired ribbon you can get a nice look by tucking the ribbon into the wreath at different spots and gluing in place . . . or you can leave the tie-ends long down the center of the wreath.

4. Glue in the stems of latafolia and cedar on each side of the bow. Be sure to push the stems way in tight to secure.

5. Glue in the stems of berries on each side of the bow. You can cut the berries in clusters if you want some short ones near the top.

6. Now cut a few leaves off the bottom of the stems of ivy to use later. Glue the remaining stems of ivy under the bow on the top, and another under the bow on the bottom. These can be bent around to achieve the desired look you want.

7. Cut the ribbon for the bells in five different lengths . . . 15″, 13″, 11″, 9″, 7″. Tie a bell onto the end of each ribbon with a slip knot. Arrange the bells in a cascade that is pleasing to you. Tie all the ends together in a single knot at the top of the ribbons. Place a wire tightly around the knot on the top of the ribbons and then wire them to the wreath under the center of the bow.

8. Tuck in the twigs and remaining ivy leaves where you think they fill in best, and glue in place (see photo).

9. Make a little nest out of the Spanish moss and glue on top of the wreath to the left side of the bow. Place a friendly little bird into the nest and glue securely. Enjoy!

Hang this on your front door for all to enjoy! You might want to frame your door with artificial Christmas greens and put big bows in the corners (to match your wreath).

A Simply Elegant Christmas

How elegant your tree will be when you decorate with a simple color scheme of white and gold, and a flock of beautiful birds. This artificial pine tree looks real once the eucalyptus twigs and baby's breath are tucked into the branches.

MATERIALS NEEDED

*Christmas tree—artificial or fresh cut
(the one pictured is an artificial 8' pine)
18 large white birds
12 small white birds
2 "grower" bunches of silver-dollar eucalyptus
1 large bunch of twigs
1 "grower" bunch of baby's breath
20–25 yards of 2½" gold ribbon
6–8 yards of ⅛" gold ribbon
10 yards of 1½" gold ribbon
5 strands of tiny white lights
(50 lights per strand)*

Note: you will use less of each item if your tree is smaller than 8' or if you only decorate the front and sides.

INSTRUCTIONS

1. The first thing to go on the tree are the lights. Intertwine them in and out of the branches. Be sure to stagger them rather than pull them tight in a straight line. Always have them plugged in while arranging them to make sure of the best placement.

2. Make the fabulous bow for the top by following the instructions on page 34 for the basic bow. This bow has ten loops on each side about 6″ long (you can make two bows with 5 loops each and then wire them together into one). Leave the tail of the ribbon 1½ times as long as the height of your tree. Tie the bow with a length of ribbon cut twice as long as the tail ribbon on the bow. When the bow is finished you will have three streamers of ribbon that are each 1½ times the height of your tree. Pull out each loop of the bow for maximum fullness.

3. Wire the bow to the top of the tree. Allow the three streamers of ribbons, evenly spaced apart, to cascade down the tree. Tuck the streamers in and out through the branches in a graceful manner (see photo for placement).

4. Tuck in the silver dollar eucalyptus all over the tree, allowing the ends to extend past the tips of the tree branches.

5. Wire the birds onto the tree in clusters. This tree has four "family groupings"...one in the front of the tree as shown in the photo—one on the left side in the upper middle of the tree—one on the back side near the top of the tree—another on the right side near the bottom of the tree to create a spiral pattern to the groupings. These "family groupings" have two large birds for Mama and Papa and three small birds for children (you might want to use the number of children in your family in the groupings).

6. Cut 1 yard of the ⅛″ gold ribbon and glue to the bottom of the beak of one large bird (leave about a 6″ tail of ribbon) and then cascade and twist it to the other large bird and glue to the bottom of the beak. Continue on to all the small birds in the grouping. Be careful not to pull tight but to let it swag. This can represent how we are all united as a family (you'll love this idea if you are a true romantic as I am). Now arrange the other large birds in pairs all over the tree and wire in place. Connect each pair by gluing a tiny gold ribbon to their beaks as well.

7. Now securely tuck in the twigs under the birds to appear as if they were resting on the twigs.

8. Make tie bows from the 1½″ gold ribbon following instructions on page 34. Use 1½–2 yards for each bow. Allow the tie ends to cascade down 12–15″ long. Place these bows randomly over the tree (I used five bows on this tree).

9. Now make small clusters of baby's breath and place at random all over the tree. Simply elegant!

This fireplace accent piece will make an impressive statement when you create this lush green look for the holidays. The design is new and unique.

You may want to string tiny white lights through the greens to give it a fantasy effect.

Create the wreath and the accent piece, then pull it all together with garland.

Christmas by the Fire

MATERIALS NEEDED

9' of artificial pine garland
grapevines
4 yards of 2" wide ribbon (the same as used for
the wreath.)

1. Hang the large wreath in the center of your mantle wall and the accent piece to the far left or right, on your mantle. Connect the two by placing the pine garland through the bottom of the wreath and draping across the mantle then behind the accent piece and down the side of the mantle. See the illustration below and the photo.

2. Twist and curl the 4 yards of ribbon through the

garland. Tuck in grapevines among the pine to complete the total look. Do not glue these in place.

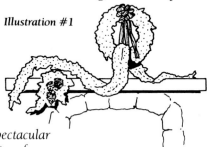

Illustration #1

You may choose to balance your spectacular
Christmas mantle with a cluster of
three cheery red candles.

Wreath

MATERIALS NEEDED

26" pine wreath—artificial or natural
6 yards of 2" wide ribbon

(if you are making the mantle side piece and garland, add another 4¾ yards)

10 large pine cones
4 stems of berries

10 large artificial holly or ivy leaves
1 small bunch of latafolia
6 stems of preserved cedar branches
1 grapevine wreath (to pull apart for the vines)
florists wire
small amounts of tiny pine cones, eucalyptus pods
and twigs

Note: If you are making the side piece and garland, be sure to purchase the materials at the same time so they all match.

INSTRUCTIONS

1. Make a large bow following the instructions on page 34. This bow has eight loops on each side about 5" long. Cut the tail ribbon 30" long. Tie the bow with a 60" length of ribbon. Pull all the ribbon ends down and cut in a V shape, leaving them as long as possible.

2. Wire and glue the bow in place on the top-center of the wreath.

3. Tuck in the large pine cones and glue firmly in place (see illustration #1).

4. Pull apart the grapevine wreath and use vine

Illustration #1

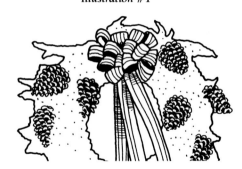

pieces of varying lengths. Tuck into the wreath and glue each end firmly in place. By using natural materials, such as vines and pine cones, your wreath will have dimension and a very natural look.

5. Glue in the ends of the latafolia and cedar. (*see illustration*).

6. Cut the berry stems to various lengths and glue in around the pine cones.

7. Now tuck in the holly or ivy leaves, tiny pine cones, eucalyptus pods, gluing as you go (see photo for placement).

Illustration #2

Accent Piece

MATERIALS NEEDED

1 block of oasis for dried arrangements
3 or 4 long stems of artificial pine branches
2 large pine cones
1 large lotus pod
4 stems of preserved cedar
2 stems of Christmas berries

5 large artificial holly or ivy leaves
¾ yards of 2″ wide ribbon
florists wire
small amounts of tiny pine cones, eucalyptus pods, twigs, Spanish moss, latafolia, and a few grapevines

INSTRUCTIONS

1. Cut the block of oasis approximately 4″× 6″ and 2″ thick to serve as a base. Completely cover this base with Spanish moss, and glue in place.

2. Glue an artificial pine branch and stem of cedar into each end of the base (see illustration #1). The arrangement in the photo measures 30″ from end to end.

3. Glue the two large pine cones and lotus pods onto the center front of the base (see illustration #1).

Illustration #1

4. Cut one or two pine and cedar branches into varying lengths and glue in around the pine cones and sides to give a nice full appearance.

5. Glue long twigs into the base in and among the long pine and cedar branches. Some of the twigs should extend out past the ends of the pine branches. Glue some short twigs around the pine cones.

6. Arrange five pieces of grapevine, approximately 15–18″ long, in a pleasing manner to add dimension to your work. Glue securely into the base (see photo for placement).

7. Glue in the berries, leaves, pods and latafolia to complete the total look of your arrangement (see photo for placement).

8. Cut three pieces of ribbon each 8″ long. Glue one end of each piece into the arrangement as shown in the photo. Cut the ends into a V.

9. Attach a piece of wire on the back for hanging.

Traditional Country Christmas

*O*h Christmas Tree, Oh Christmas Tree, how lovely are your branches. . . . Your guests will be enchanted when they see your spectacular traditional Christmas Tree. Your room will come alive with the spirit of Christmas, as your family gathers around this beautiful tree aglow with hundreds of tiny white lights. This tree has a number of unique decorative features. . . from the wonderful twig and berry garland, to the delicate covering of baby's breath. You may want to pick just two or three of these ideas to try on your tree this year, adding new things in the years to come.

MATERIALS NEEDED

Find as large a Christmas Tree as your room will hold. The one pictured is a fresh cut 11' Douglas fir. Be sure to choose a tree that is nicely shaped and full enough that you can't see through it.

Tiny white lights
The 11' tree in the photo has 8 strands with 50 lights on each strand.

Twig garland
Can be grapevine, birch, twigs, etc. They are wired together to make a garland. This tree has three 10'

Berry garland
This is made by wiring berry stems together.

Red, green, gold shiny ball ornaments
This tree has 3 dozen of each color.

Red ribbon, 1" wide for tying ornament clusters.
I used 18 yards for 3 dozen ornament clusters (or 6 yards per 1 dozen ornament clusters).

Large angel for the top of the tree

Wired red ribbon for bows
I used 24 bows with 1 yard for each bow.

Unique ornaments you or the children have made or collected through the years.

Icicles—large clear
I used 3 dozen on this size tree.

Baby's breath
4 full "grower" bunches were used on this tree.

INSTRUCTIONS
Make some popcorn, put on the Christmas music and have a wonderful time decorating your tree.

1. Always place the lights on your tree—first thing. Intertwine them in and out of the branches. Be sure to stagger them rather than pull them tight in a straight line. Always have them plugged in while arranging them to make sure they are evenly spaced throughout the tree. (Instructions continued on next page . . .)

2. Now place the large angel on top.

3. Next to go on your tree should be the garland. If you are using grapevines, place three vines together to make the garland thick (no need to wire these together, just tuck them snugly into the tree branches, adding new lengths of vines as you go along). If you are using shorter twigs such as birch, wire about 10 branches together in bundles and then wire the bundles together to make 3 or 4 garlands, each 6 to 10′ long (see illustration #1).

Illustration #1

4. Start the placement of the garland at the side of the tree on the bottom and drape it through the branches of the tree as illustrated below (see illustration #2).

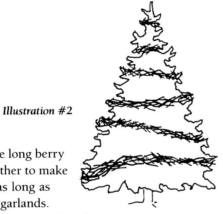

Illustration #2

5. Wire the long berry stems together to make a garland as long as your twig garlands. Intertwine these berries along with the twigs on your tree. This will give your tree a unique natural look.

6. Cluster the shiny ball ornaments by tying one red, one green and one gold ornament together with ½ yard of 1″ red ribbon. Tie a bow on the top of each

cluster and hang them on your tree with an ornament hook. Distribute the clusters evenly over the entire tree. You will achieve depth and dimension by placing some clusters at the ends of branches and others closer to the tree trunk.

7. Make tie bows following instructions on page 33 from 1 yard of wired ribbon. Bend the tails of the bows and cut the ends on the diagonal as illustrated. Place bows evenly all over your tree at the ends of the branches (see illustration #3).

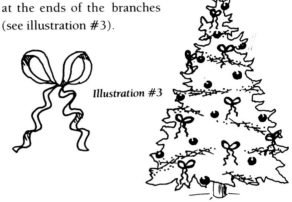

Illustration #3

8. Arrange the wonderful unique ornaments you have collected throughout the years all over your tree. My children are grown, but what sweet memories I have when I place on my tree each year the ornaments they made when they were young. These will give the tree your own special personality.

9. I like to hang clear icicles from the ends of the branches to glisten in the light.

10. Now for the grand finale...tuck in stems of baby's breath all over your tree for a fairytale look of fresh snowflakes. The baby's breath will slowly dry on your tree and will still look nice 2–3 weeks later. If you are having a special party, plan to put on the baby's breath the day before for the best visual impact. You can place some in the greens on your mantle or table to tie in the feeling.

Presents Under the Tree

Oh how my family loves Christmas! My talented daughter, Julie McGaha, goes all out to make her gift packages special for her handsome husband and two adorable boys. This year she had fun wrapping all her gifts alike for a great look under the tree! Some of the packages she sent home to us are shown in the center of the photo, all tied with shiny gold ribbon.

I always wrap my gifts in coordinating companion papers and tie them all with Christmas red ribbon. Use different types of bows to complement the size of the box.

A Touch of Glass

Your glass hurricane lamp will take on an extra special flair when you add a festive wreath around the middle.

MATERIALS NEEDED

florists wire
3 yards of ¼" ribbon
small amount of Spanish moss, German statice,
latafolia, artificial pine, preserved cedar, artificial
ivy or small ivy leaves, berries and tiny pine cones

INSTRUCTIONS

1. Make a circle of wire to fit around the center of your hurricane lamp. Twist the wire together to hold firmly. Completely cover the wire by wrapping it with Spanish moss.

2. Wrap the ribbon around the Spanish moss and wire to hold it all in place. Allow about 1½" of Spanish moss between each loop of ribbon, being careful not to pull the ribbon too tight. Tie the ribbon ends onto the wreath to hold in place.

3. Make a bow following the instructions for basic bow on page 34. This bow has five loops on each side about 2" long. Cut the tail of the ribbon 7" long. Tie the bow with a piece of ribbon cut 15" long.

4. Tie and glue the bow onto the wire wreath. Glue in two lengths of ribbon about 8" long under the bottom of the bow so that you will have five ribbon ends coming down from the bow. Cut the ribbon ends diagonally at varying lengths.

5. Securely glue small pieces of German statice and greens into the Spanish moss, completely covering the wreath. These pieces should be small, as large ones will pull down the moss.

6. Arrange the berries, tiny pine cones, latafolia and leaves completely around the wreath and glue firmly into the Spanish moss. Your wreath will be most attractive if it has a free flowing, high-low feeling...so don't press these materials too closely together.

7. Place your wreath over the hurricane lamp with the bow on the side.

Now place your hurricane lamp over a large scented
candle and enjoy this unique look. You can
make another wreath for spring by
gluing silk flower blossoms and ivy leaves instead of
Christmas greens and berries.

Memories of Christmas

*Fill a beautiful basket with Christmas cards from special friends
as a wonderful centerpiece for your dining table.*

MATERIALS NEEDED

*1 large attractive basket
1 24" length of silk pine garland
2 long stems of holly berries and leaves
3 long stems of preserved cedar
3 yards of wired ribbon
3/4 yard of gold braid*

INSTRUCTIONS

1. Attach the pine garland to the handle and let it cascade down the left side of the basket. Glue in place.

2. Make the basic bow with the three loops on each side approximately 4" long (see instructions on page 34). Leave the tail of the bow 16" long. Tie the bow with a length of ribbon cut 18" long. Wire and glue the bow onto the pine garland and basket handle on the left side, allowing the long ribbon to cascade down. Cut a length of ribbon 20" long. Glue it under the bow and twist it through the pine across the top of the handle. Bend the shorter tie ends in a pleasing manner to the front and back of the bow.

3. Make a simple tie bow from the gold braid (see instructions on page 33). Tie a knot 3" from each end and unravel the braid to create a tassel. Glue into the center of the large bow.

4. Glue a stem of holly berries and a stem of cedar on each side of the bow. Arrange in and around the pine for a natural flow. Glue a cedar branch in front under the bow.

*Place this beautiful basket on your dining table, add some brass candlesticks.
Fill with cards to enjoy as a daily reminder of all the best wishes
from your special friends!*

Sweet Scents of Christmas

Your kitchen will take on the wonderful scent of Christmas when you fill this darling basket with Christmas potpourri. The festive decoration and bow will add the final charming touch. Place it on your kitchen counter or window sill, anywhere you will be sure to enjoy it (you may also use the basket to hold your Christmas cards).

MATERIALS NEEDED

small basket with handle (this one is 8 × 10 oval)

6 yards of 1″ wide ribbon

small amounts of latafolia, preserved cedar,

preserved fern, german statice, white flower

statice, berries, tiny pine cones,

Christmas potpourri

INSTRUCTIONS

1. Make the basic bow following instructions on page 34. This bow has five loops on each side about 3″ long. Cut the tail about 5″ long. Tie the bow with a 12″ length of ribbon pulling one end up and the other end down.

2. Glue the bow to the basket at the base of the handle. Pull two ribbon ends down and the other one at the top is arranged and glued across the basket handle as shown in the photo.

3. Glue one end of the length of ribbon remaining up under the bottom of the bow on the left side. Bring the ribbon down the left side of the basket and twist and

curl completely around the basket edge, gluing as you go to hold it in place. Glue the end of the ribbon under the right side of the bow. For the most attractive look, create a lot of highs and lows when arranging the ribbon rather than pulling too tightly or straight.

4. Glue onto the basket, under and around the bow, all the greens, flowers, berries and pine cones as shown in the photo.

5. Crumple paper to fill in the bottom of the basket up to near the top. This way you won't have to use so much potpourri. Now place a heavy layer of potpourri over the paper in the basket and enjoy!

This basket is adorable and easy to make so put together several to give as gifts.

Deck the Walls

The gold bells will glisten in the candlelight as this beautiful wreath adorns your dining room wall.

MATERIALS NEEDED

large artificial pine wreath (this one is 24″ across)
7 large pine cones
7 small clusters of berries
1 small bunch of preserved cedar
small amount of latafolia
5 large gold jingle bells
6 yards of 2½″ wide ribbon
2 yards of ½″ wide ribbon for bells (if you can't
find the narrow ribbon to match the wide ribbon
you can use solid red or green)
7 large artificial holly leaves or ivy
small amount of spanish moss and twigs
bird
wire

INSTRUCTIONS

1. Make a basic bow following instructions on page 34 with five loops on each side about 6″ long, leaving the tail 19″ long. Wire your bow. Tie the bow with a length of ribbon cut 32″ long, leaving the end at the top of the bow about 6″ long and the end at the bottom of the bow about 26″ long.

2. Wire and glue the bow in place on the wreath to the upper left side. Pull the 6″ ribbon tail on the bow to the outside of the wreath and the 26″ ribbon tail across the middle of the wreath to reach the other side and glue in place. The great thing about this wired ribbon is that you can bend it easily into any shape you like. Follow the flow of the ribbon shown in the photo if you like this free flowing look. Pull the 19″ long ribbon tail to the right side of the bow and arrange into the wreath, glue ends to hold. Cut a length of ribbon 19″ long and glue one end on the left side of the bow. Arrange into the wreath and glue in place.

3. Cut the ribbon for bells into five different lengths . . . 15″, 13″, 11″, 9″, 7″. Tie a bell onto the end of each ribbon using a slip knot. Arrange the bells in a cascade that is pleasing to you. Tie all the ribbon ends together in a single knot at the top. Place a wire securely around the knot on the top of the ribbons and then wire them onto the wreath under the bow. Let them cascade down the wreath.

4. Arrange the seven large pine cones on the wreath, pushing them snugly into the greens, and glue securely in place (see illustration #1 for placement).

5. Attach the preserved cedar to the wreath with glue and push ends way into the greens to secure (see illustration #1).

Illustration #1

6. Glue the seven small clusters of berries and holly leaves onto the wreath as shown in photo.

7. Make a birds nest out of spanish moss and glue into the pine wreath on the middle right side. Glue the bird into the nest (it will help secure the bird if you wrap the wire on the feet of the bird around a pine branch on the wreath).

8. Now glue in place the latafolia, twigs and small pine cones (see photo for placement). An artificial wreath will look most realistic when you add these natural items plus it will give depth and dimension to your work.

Enjoy!

Warm Glow of Christmas

You will enjoy this beautiful arrangement in the center of your table as your family and friends gather around for a festive Christmas dinner.

MATERIALS NEEDED

basket (the one pictured is 6 × 10″)
oasis for dried arrangements
4 large pine cones
9 small pine cones
2 lotus pods
12 artificial pine branches
2 stems of small leaf ivy
12 large ivy leaves
1 bunch of preserved cedar
twigs
berries–2 long stems, 3 short stems
spanish moss
2 birds

INSTRUCTIONS

1. Cut the oasis to firmly fit the basket and glue to the bottom.

2. Securely glue into the oasis, 9 branches of artificial pine and 5 branches of cedar (see illustration #1 for placement).

3. Arrange the four large pine cones as shown in the illustration and firmly glue in place.

Illustration #1

4. Cut three stems of artificial pine in varying shorter lengths and glue into the oasis all the way around the arrangement to the desired fullness. IMPORTANT . . . leave a circle in the center to position the candle securely on the oasis.

5. Now glue in two long stems of ivy, one on each end and bend to desired position. Arrange the 12 large ivy leaves among the pine branches, emphasizing the right side to balance the pine cones that are on the left.

6. Arrange the two long stems of berries and the three shorter clusters on the right side of the arrangement as shown in the photo. Note: One short berry cluster is on the back side of the arrangement.

7. Tuck in the nine small pine cones around the bottom of the large pine cones and glue in place. Note: Be sure to complete the arrangement on the back side.

8. Make two small birds nests from the spanish moss and tuck them into the greens, one on each side of the arrangement. Glue in place.

9. Place a friendly bird into each nest, gluing securely.

10. Tuck one lotus pod into the greenery to the left of each nest and glue.

11. Arrange the wispy twigs in an attractive manner to give your arrangement a natural woodsy look (see photo for placement).

12. Place a large red Christmas candle in the center.

May the cheery glow from the candle centerpiece brighten your Christmas dinner festivities.

Christmas Morning

The charming look of a Christmas Tree loaded with toys and packages brings back many childhood memories. This unique adorable wreath will delight the child in all of us.

MATERIALS NEEDED

vine wreath (this one is 12″ across)

small artificial Christmas Tree to fit in the center

small toys and packages to fit under the tree

6 yards of ½″ wide ribbon

½ yard of ⅛″ ribbon

small amounts of spanish moss, tiny white flowers,

latafolia, tiny red flowers or berries, tiny pine cones

INSTRUCTIONS

1. Securely glue the Christmas Tree into the middle of your wreath by removing the wooden tree base and pushing the wire tree trunk into the vines of the wreath. Arrange the branches of the tree to be full in the front and sides and flat across the back.

2. Glue spanish moss around the wire trunk and under the base of the tree.

3. Twist and curl the ribbon all the way around the wreath as shown in the photo, gluing as you go. Be careful not to use a lot of glue on the ribbon as it sometimes will show through. It is best to apply the glue in a fold or other place that would hide the glue spot.

4. Make a basic bow as per the instructions on page 34. This bow has five loops on each side about 3″ long.

Leave the ribbon tail about 5″ long. Tie the bow with a 12″ length of ribbon.

5. Glue the bow to the wreath on the bottom, just to the left of the center. Cut two lengths of ribbon each about 6″ long and glue one end of each ribbon up under the bottom of the bow. Pull all five ribbon tail ends down and cut on the diagonal.

6. Make a mini tie bow of ⅛″ ribbon, following instructions on page 33 and glue to the top of your tiny tree.

7. Arrange tiny flowers or berries and pine cones on the tree as shown in the photo and glue in place.

8. Securely glue the small packages and toys under and around the base of the tree.

Place this wreath in a spot where the children can see the detail and enjoy!

Santa Candy Jar

This adorable Santa has watched over the festivities in our home ever since my children were young. They were delighted when I included him in this book!

MATERIALS NEEDED

brandy glass 4½" tall, 3¼" across the largest part

2–12" red felt squares

12" × 1" strip of white fake fur

2–½" red pom pom balls for buttons

1–1" red pom pom ball

3½" styrofoam ball

6" long strip of white fringe for beard

small amount of white felt for mittens, black felt

for eyes and boots

INSTRUCTIONS
Pattern on page 68

For Santa's Body:

1. Trace the pattern for Santa's coat and cut it out of red felt. Place the coat around the brandy glass as shown in the photo and glue onto the glass only at the end of each sleeve.

2. Trace the pattern for mittens and cut them out of white felt. Glue onto the glass, slightly overlapping the sleeve ends of the coat.

3. Trace the boot pattern and cut them out of black felt. Glue onto the glass base as shown in the photo.

4. Glue the small red pom poms in the middle of the glass for buttons (shown in photo).

For Santa's Hat and Head:

1. Trace the pattern for Santa's hat. The page was not long enough to accommodate the actual pattern so you will need to extend it ½" on each end for the full size needed for the hat. Cut the hat out of red felt.

2. Glue the red felt hat around the top of the styrofoam ball (hot glue will melt the styrofoam so use white glue). Fold the felt point over the top of the ball and glue securely, holding in place with a straight pin. Now glue a large red pom pom over this spot.

3. Glue the white fringe onto the ball to form the beard (see photo). The fringe ends should come up to the felt hat on each side.

4. Glue the strip of white fake fur around the bottom of the felt hat (be sure to cover the ends of the fringe).

5. Glue the tiny gold ball into the styrofoam for the nose.

6. Cut the black felt for eyes. Trace the eye pattern for cutting lines. Glue in place.

7. Put a little of your own powder blush on Santa's cheeks to make them rosy.

Fill the glass with Christmas candy and place the head on top to complete Santa!

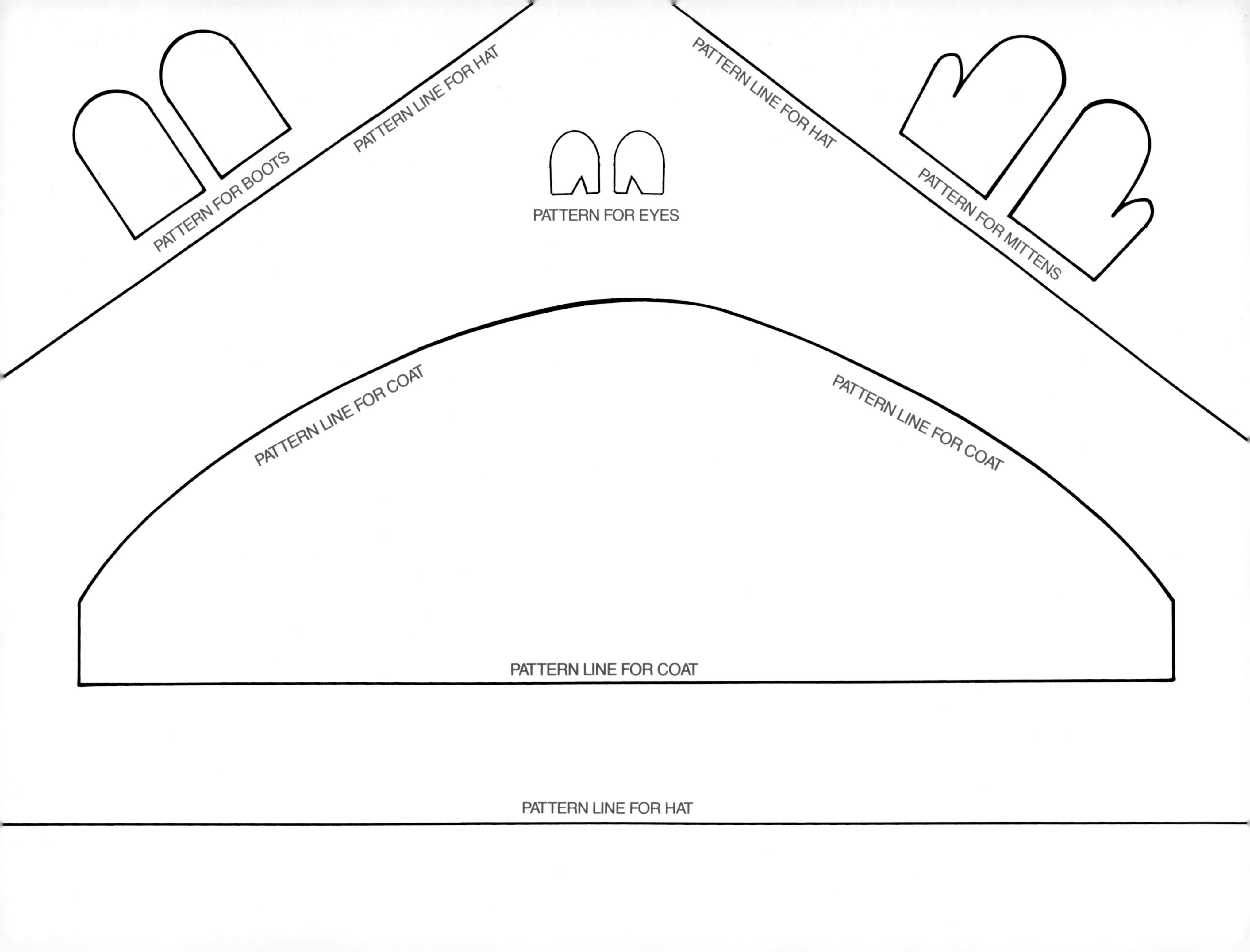

PATTERN FOR MITTENS

PATTERN LINE FOR HAT

PATTERN LINE FOR COAT

PATTERN LINE FOR COAT

PATTERN LINE FOR HAT

PATTERN FOR EYES

PATTERN LINE FOR COAT

PATTERN LINE FOR COAT

PATTERN LINE FOR HAT

PATTERN LINE FOR HAT

PATTERN FOR BOOTS

Jingle Bell

You'll enjoy the cheery jingle sound every time you open your kitchen cabinet with this lovely jingle bell.

MATERIALS NEEDED

1 large gold jingle bell
1½ yards of 1" wide ribbon
1 tiny piece of artificial pine
a few berries, fruit and tiny pine cones

INSTRUCTIONS

1. Make the basic bow following instructions on page 34. This bow has three loops on each side about 3" long. Cut the tail even with the end of the loop. Staple the bow together in the center.

2. Pull the remaining ribbon (about ½ yard) through the ring on top of the bell and even up the ends. Tie the bow onto the bell with this ribbon. The bow should rest on the ring on top of the bell. Tie the ribbon tightly round the bow then pull the ribbon ends up together and tie in a slip knot. This forms the loop for hanging.

3. Glue one end of the tiny pine piece (about 1½–2" long) to the top of the bow knot.

4. Glue the berries, fruit and tiny pine cones to the top of the bow knot.

Be ready to make more, as everyone will want one!

The Grand Ball

This festive Christmas decoration will delight your friends and add to the holiday atmosphere in your home.

MATERIALS NEEDED

1 extra large shiny plastic Christmas ball (the photo shows a 10" ball)
1 clear plastic dish or saucer proportioned to the ball
(a 7" dish was used here)
³/₄ yard of 1¹/₂" wide wired ribbon
12" of decorative red or gold wire
1 spray of silk holly leaves
Several stems of preserved cedar or other greens
6 short stems of silk pine greens
Small amounts of berries, tiny pinecones and moss

INSTRUCTIONS

1. Turn the clear plastic dish upside down. Hot glue the Christmas ball in the center of the dish, positioning the stem of the ball on the top, slightly to the right.

2. Completely cover the dish with moss and glue to hold. Glue a small amount of moss over the stem at the top of the ball.

3. Cut the silk pine branches in varying lengths and glue around the base of the ball. The longer branches should extend out to the right side. Glue a few pine branches into the moss around the stem on top of the ball, allowing a longer branch to extend to the left side.

4. Glue a few branches of preserved cedar into the moss on top of the ball. Extend one branch out and slightly down the left side of the ball and another up and out on the top right. This is to balance your arrangement.

5. Make a tie bow of wired ribbon following instructions on page 33 and glue to the top of the ball. The wire in the ribbon allows you to bend the ends any way you like.

6. Tuck in the silk holly leaves, berries, pinecones and extra greens around the bow and also to the base of the ball. Glue to hold in place.

7. Bend the red or gold wire to form a large loop and glue into the moss around the stem to resemble a Christmas ornament hanger (this is optional).

This ball would be a great gift for a special friend.

Tahoe Pines

We had such fun picking up pine cones at Lake Tahoe. Look at how adorable they are all decorated for Christmas.

MATERIALS NEEDED

*1 nicely shaped large pine cone
1 small bird
small amount of artificial Christmas greens, tiny
pine cones, berries and fruit
2½ yards of 1″ wide ribbon*

INSTRUCTIONS

1. Cut the pine branches into short sections of varying lengths and arrange them on the top of the pine cone. Glue in place (see photo for placement).

2. Glue the bird in among the greens.

3. Glue tiny pine cones, berries and fruit into the greens.

4. Cut a 30″ length of ribbon and glue securely on each side of the pine cone. This becomes the handle for hanging.

5. Make a basic bow following instructions on page 34. This bow has three loops on each side about 3″ long. Cut the tail about 6″ long. Tie the bow with a 12″ length of ribbon. Glue to the pine cone on the right side (see photo for placement).